Marvin the Math Cat

& Dusty's Secret Quest

H & N Blackburn

Blackburn Alliance

Book Cover and Illustrations by H & N Blackburn

Contents

Dedicated to all children, parents, and teachers seeking the usefulness of math and its real-world applications. May this book inspire you to embrace the power of numbers and embark on your own mathematical adventures.

Marvin the Math Cat & Dusty's Secret Quest

MARVIN NERVOUSLY TAPPED HIS paw on his desk as he and Dusty sat on stools, chatting quietly while they waited for Mrs. Catnip to return their graded math quizzes. The rest of the class was doing the same, the only sounds coming from the teacher's footsteps as she made her way around the room.

"I bet you aced it again, Marvin," Dusty said, grinning in his direction.

"I hope you're right," Marvin replied, his voice a little shaky with nerves.

Dusty shrugged. "I'm not sure how well *I* did. I struggled with some of those geometry questions."

Mrs. Catnip reached Marvin's desk and placed his quiz face-down. "Very well done, Marvin!" she said with a smile.

Marvin took a deep breath and flipped the sheet over, scanning the perfect score. His eyes widened in disbelief as he realized he had aced his geometry math quiz, answering every question correctly. A rush of joy spread across his face, whisker to whisker. When he turned to share his excitement with Dusty, he noticed Dusty's downcast expression.

"What's wrong?" Marvin asked, concerned.

"Oh, nothing. Just a bit upset that I got some wrong," Dusty answered in a hushed tone.

"Let me see." Marvin took the paper from Dusty's paws and examined it closely. "Hmm, well, you missed a few things in the transformations section. For one thing, you didn't rotate the triangle the right amount," he pointed out.

"I see what you mean. How did you learn this so well?" Dusty asked, "I still find this confusing in my head."

"Remember the patio garden I designed?" Marvin asked, a mischievous gleam in his eye.

"Yeah, the one from your dream," Dusty chuckled.

"It wasn't a dream. I was there, and so were you, I think."

Dusty raised an eyebrow skeptically. "That seems strange to me, but if it helped you ace your math quiz, maybe you have a special friend helping you learn math. Or, maybe it has to do with the Geomath Landscaping cats?"

Marvin nodded, recalling the odd cats they had encountered while walking home from school. "Interesting point. I'm still puzzled by the landscaping cats as well. They weren't even dressed appropriately for working in someone's backyard — sunglasses and ties. What's that about?"

"I know, very strange. But they do good work! You saw the new patio garden they designed for us. It's very nice!" Dusty said with excitement.

"Yes, and it looks exactly like the one I designed," Marvin whispered to himself.

"What did you say?" Dusty asked, curious.

"Nothing," Marvin said, shaking his head. "Class is almost over. Let's go get some lunch."

"Okay," Dusty replied. But something still bothered Dusty about Marvin's "dream." With their combined creativity and Marvin's sleuthing skills, he hoped they could figure it out before it figured them out.

LATER THAT DAY, DUSTY sat on one of the cozy cat benches in his backyard patio garden, waiting for Marvin to finish his supper so they could go out and play. His parents had recently gifted him a smartphone which he was only supposed to use to call them, but Dusty couldn't resist the lure of social media. He opened Catbook and scrolled through some of his classmates' posts. As he scrolled, he began to feel unusually sleepy. *Why am I so tired?* he thought. *Maybe I'll take a short catnap*. Dusty closed his eyes and slinked down onto the hard bench surface, sprawling out so that the blue umbrella partially covered his body. He placed his phone on the bench beside him and drifted off to sleep.

But Dusty's nap was cut short by an alarming sound from his phone. "Beeeeeep, Beeeeeep! Beeeeeep, Beeeeeep!" Dusty picked up his phone to silence the noise. It was an alarm, but he didn't remember setting it. As he unlocked his phone, he noticed a new application on his Home Screen. The icon for the app showed a central white circle with three smaller light-colored circles surrounding it, connected by an orbiting curved line. The background behind the symbol was a radiant blue with tiny sparkling white dots, which gave the appearance of light glistening off new-fallen snow.

I don't remember installing this app, Dusty thought. His cat curiosity enticed him to open the application. He needed to know what it was about and delete it if it was useless.

Inside the app, an image appeared on screen — a map of Purrfect Paradise! Below the map, he saw a few paragraphs of text and a "Next" button:

Welcome to the ICAP Math Quest! This quest will help you apply your math skills to solve real-world problems and learn more about us.

After completing the quest, you will be rewarded with a clue to the next stage.

Dusty's mind was racing with questions. *What was this math quest? Who was behind it? Why was he chosen to participate?* He continued reading, but the words only added to his confusion.

There is one thing you must promise as you journey on your quest. Keep this to yourself, don't even tell your best friend. The reason will reveal itself at the end.

Click Next to open a math problem for the location of your first clue.

Dusty wondered why he couldn't share this quest with Marvin. They were best friends, after all. He almost decided not to go through with it, but his curiosity got the better of him, and he clicked the Next button.

The app presented him with the first math problem:

Problem #1:
It takes the planet Meowcury 88 days to make one revolution around the Sun. How many days does it take Meowcury to make two revolutions around the Sun?

Dusty sighed. He wasn't very good at math, but he had a feeling this had something to do with the Geomath Landscaping cats, so he decided to give it a try. Then, he would hopefully be able to tell Marvin about his experience. He popped a fish-flavored breath mint into his mouth to help him concentrate and got to work.

Dusty knew that Meowcury was the smallest planet closest to the Sun. If it took 88 days for it to make one revolution, it would take twice that long for it to make two revolutions. He mentally added 88 and 88 by adding 80 and 80 to get 160, then added 8 and 8 to get 16, and finally, added 160 and 16 to get 176.

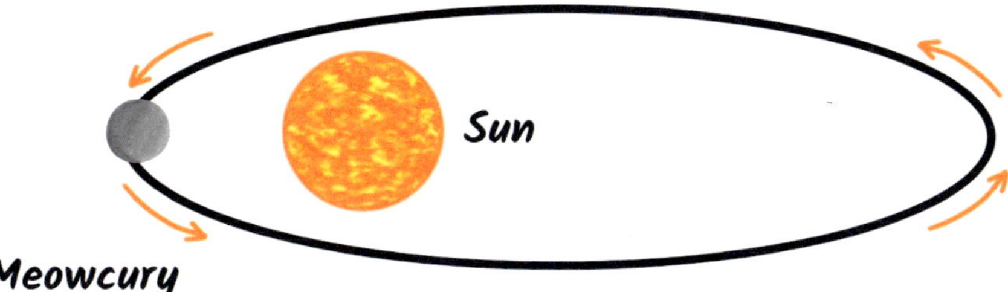

Takes 88 days to make one revolution

2 revolutions = 88 + 88

Mental Math: 80 + 80 = 160

8 + 8 = 16

So, 160 + 16 = 176 days

That's it! Dusty thought. *It takes 176 days for Meowcury to make two revolutions around the Sun*!

Dusty's nimble paws typed his answer into the space provided, and with a confident click of the submit button, he waited for the app's response. Suddenly, a grey Question Mark icon appeared on the map at the location of the Town Hall.

He zoomed in to get a better look.

Dusty felt a surge of pride as he submitted his answer on the Math Quest app. He had gotten it right! Maybe he could solve all the clues on his own, after all. But it was getting late, and he had to stop for the day. He figured the location of the first clue must be where the grey Question Mark icon had appeared on the map.

As he was thinking, Marvin walked in through the patio door. “Hi, Marvin,” Dusty said, closing the app on his phone and putting it down on the bench.

“Hey, what’s up?” Marvin asked.

“Oh, not much. I was just browsing Catbook,” Dusty replied, feeling a little guilty for keeping his math quest a secret from Marvin. But he didn’t want to give up just yet.

“How about we go to the playground downtown?” Marvin suggested.

“Sure, that sounds like fun,” Dusty said, but his mind was still on the math quest. He knew he needed to find a way to keep Marvin from finding out about it. As they walked together to the sidewalk, Dusty pondered different strategies he could use.

THE NEXT DAY DUSTY woke up early and jumped out of bed. He stretched his back by extending his front paws on the floor and scampered downstairs, where his mother was tidying up the kitchen, preparing for brunch.

"Morning Dusty, where are you running off to?" his mom asked.

"Oh, nowhere. I have to go find something," he replied before darting out the front door.

"Don't forget we're having brunch today. Be back soon!" she called out after him with a sigh.

Dusty headed straight for the Purrfect Paradise Town Hall, passing several houses in his neighborhood before veering toward Main Street. He eventually arrived at a large, looming building with an arching doorway — the Town Hall.

Checking his phone's map, he saw that the grey Question Mark icon was still showing at the Town Hall but wasn't clickable. He decided to walk around the building. As he passed a giant statue of the founding cat of Purrfect Paradise, Mr. Miceman, the icon turned bright red and became active on his screen, triggering another math problem to appear.

Problem #2:

Imagine you are on a spaceship traveling from your home planet, Purrth, to the Sun. The distance between Purrth and the Sun is 93,000,000 miles and is called an Astronomical Unit (AU). Astronomical Units are used to measure distances in space.

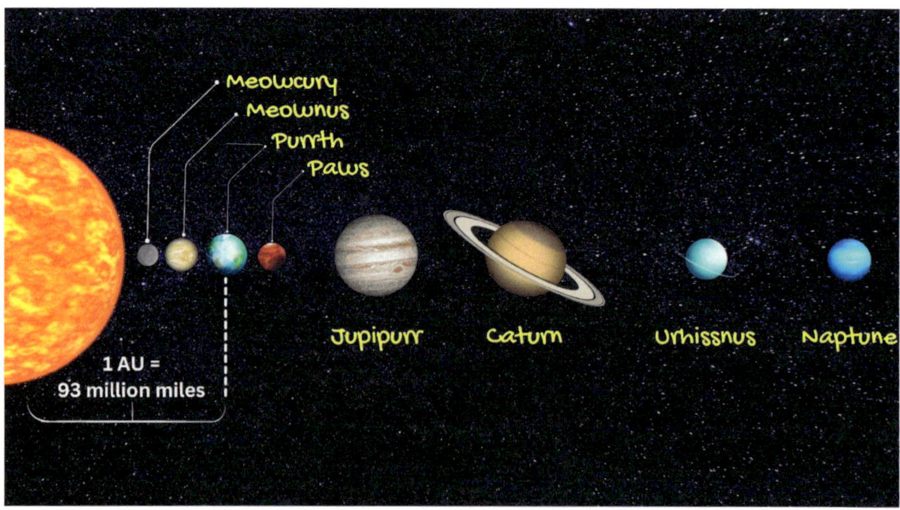

a. If the planet Jupipurr is 5 AU from the Sun, how many miles is this?

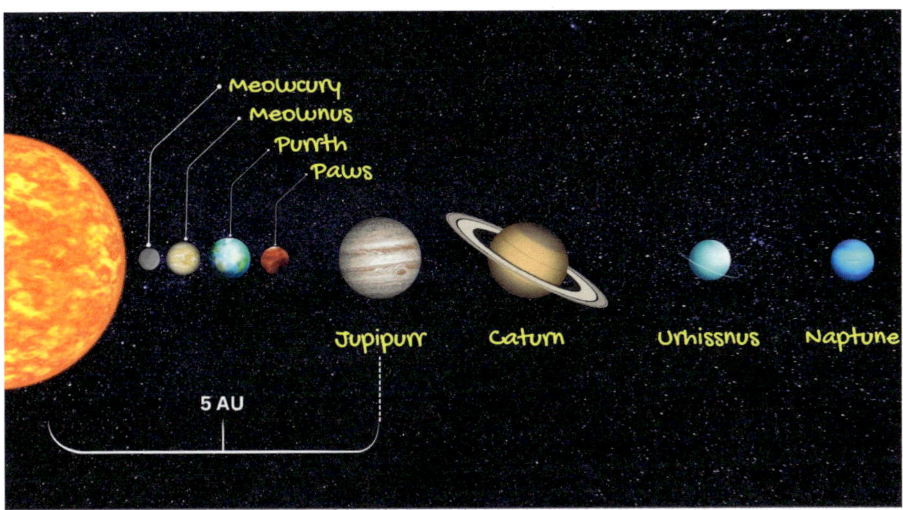

b. If Caturn is 886 million miles away from the Sun, how many AU is this? Round your answer to one decimal place.

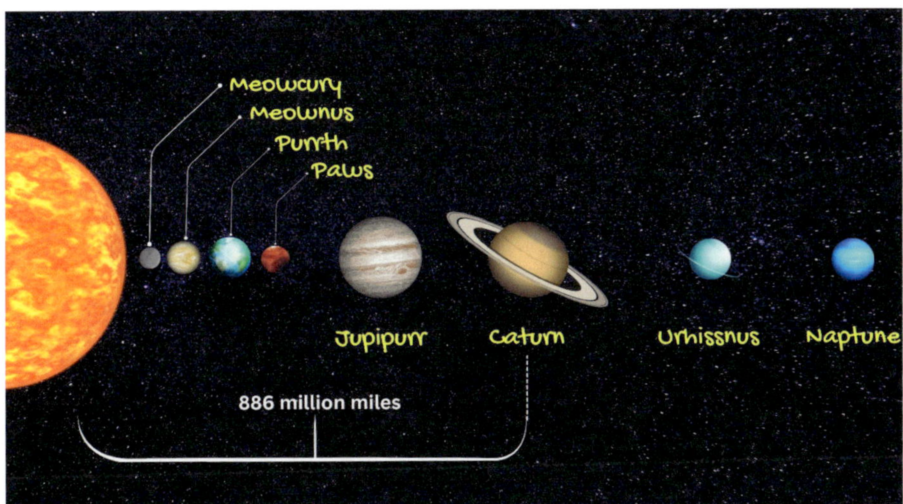

Dusty thought to himself, *Hmmm... What's with the astronomy theme? This problem seems a lot harder. I wonder if I can search for things I don't*

understand on my phone. He continued to think about how to solve the math problem in hopes that he could solve it before returning home.

> **a.** If the planet Jupipurr is 5 AU from the Sun, how many miles is this?

Okay, so in question a., I have to figure out how many miles are equivalent to 5 Astronomical Units or AU. I've never heard of this unit of measure before, but it is interesting that because distances are so large in space, they would use the distance between Purrth and the Sun as a standard. The problem says 1 AU = 93 million miles, so if we have 5 AU, wouldn't I multiply this number by 5? I think that makes sense because Jupipurr is much further away from the Sun than Purrth! Dusty opened the calculator app on his phone and began typing numbers:

$$93{,}000{,}000\, miles/AU \times 5\ AU = 465{,}000{,}000\ miles$$

Dusty looked at the answer and thought, *That is a huge number! There are six zeros, meaning it can be read as 465 million miles.*

Satisfied he had solved part a, he proceeded to question b:

> **b.** If Caturn is 886 million miles away from the Sun, how many AU is this? Round your answer to one decimal place.

For the next question, it wants me to do the opposite and calculate the number of AU for a specific distance expressed in miles. So, Caturn is 886 million miles away, which would be 886,000,000 miles. How do I calculate AU from this? Oh, wait! The information in the problem indicates that 1 AU = 93,000,000 miles. So, wouldn't I do the reverse operation and divide 886 million miles by 93 million miles/AU to get the distance in Astronomical Units? I think so!

Maybe I should start by setting up a proportion or equation that represents two equivalent ratios to help me work out the steps:

$$\frac{93{,}000{,}000\ miles}{1\ AU} = \frac{886{,}000{,}000\ miles}{?\ AU}$$

Since there is an equal sign, both sides of the equation must equal 93 million because, on the left side, 93 million divided by 1 equals 93 million. Therefore, 886 million divided by our unknown, on the right side of the equation, must also equal 93 million. So, what can I multiply by in the numerator (top number) and denominator (bottom number) of the fraction on the left-hand side to find the answer? Hmm...going back to what I was thinking earlier, if I divide 886 million by 93 million, that should tell me what factor to use. Let me try it and see if it makes sense.

$$\frac{886{,}000{,}000}{93{,}000{,}000}$$

$$= 9.52688$$

$$\sim 9.5$$

Therefore, 9.52688 or 9.5 is the factor I need to multiply 1 AU by in the denominator to determine how many Astronomical Units are equivalent to 886 million miles. My initial thought was correct: I would just be doing the reverse operation and dividing the distance a planet is from the Sun in miles by 93 million miles (= 1 AU) to find out the distance in Astronomical Units.

$$\frac{93{,}000{,}000\ miles \times 9.5}{1\ AU \times 9.5} = \frac{886{,}000{,}000\ miles}{9.5\ AU}$$

Yes! This makes sense to me! Caturn is 9.5 AU away from the Sun. Yay! I think I'm starting to get this stuff!

He typed his answers into the spaces provided in the Math Quest app and shut his eyes tightly as he clicked Submit. Very slowly, he opened his eyes, just a sliver at first. The words on the screen read Congratulations! Phew, he succeeded! He was now two for two and felt proud of his progress.

Like before, another grey Question Mark icon appeared on the map, beckoning him to continue the quest. He couldn't resist the urge to solve another math problem but realized he would be late for brunch if he didn't hurry back soon. Hoping Marvin would be able to join them today, he reluctantly closed the Math Quest app and scampered back to his home.

THE SCREEN DOOR CREAKED as Dusty bounded into the house and jumped into his chair. "You're late!" his mother said as she placed a plate of fluffy mice-flavored pancakes or *mice cakes* in front of him.

"Sorry!" Dusty said as he gulped down a big bite and gazed at his mother's glistening eyes.

Dusty's mother settled into her chair across from his father, and they ate silently until they were startled by a knock at the door.

"Hi, everyone, room for one more?" Marvin said through the screen door.

"Sure!" Dusty's parents said in unison.

Marvin took a seat and began to eat his mice cakes.

"Where did you go this morning? I saw you running out the door earlier," Marvin asked Dusty.

"Oh, I had to go check on something downtown for...ahhh...for ahh...well, it's nothing really...I'll tell you later," he stammered.

"Okay..." Marvin said suspiciously.

"So, what should we do today?" Dusty asked, trying to change the subject.

"Hmm...I'm not sure," Marvin replied.

"Well, the big spring dance-a-thon is coming up in a few weeks. We should find dance partners to make it more fun! What do you think?" Dusty proposed as he looked at Marvin's worried expression.

"What's the dance-a-thon all about?" Dusty's mother asked with curiosity. She glanced at his father, who was engrossed in his food and seemed not to be listening.

"It's a fundraiser for the school. The idea is to dance as long as you can, and the cats who dance the longest win prizes. They're selling tickets too so that you can come and watch, Mom," Dusty explained.

"That sounds like a lot of fun, Dusty. Your father and I would be happy to come along and support you," Dusty's mother said, looking in his father's direction.

"Yes, it would be entertaining to watch. I'm sure you and Marvin will win something!" Dusty's father said, looking up from his plate of mice cakes.

"Don't you remember coming to the one last year?" Dusty asked his parents, puzzled.

"Oh, you're right. We did watch a dance event you were in last year. I didn't realize it was the same thing," Dusty's mother said.

Hoping to avoid the dance-a-thon this year, Marvin looked up from his plate and confessed, "Honestly, I'm not much of a dancer. I have four left feet."

Dusty laughed, "Don't worry. I'm sure you'll do great, especially if you have a good dance partner."

"I hope you're right," Marvin said.

"Do you have anyone in mind?" Dusty coaxed.

"Maybe, I'll have to think about it," Marvin said.

Dusty thought to himself that this would be perfect. If Marvin was distracted by the need to find a dance partner for the dance-a-thon, he could finish the quest without Marvin finding out!

After eating, they licked and cleaned their paws and faces, as all cats with good hygiene should, and strolled out of Dusty's front door towards downtown.

"Let's stop by the Suit Yourself clothing store to see if they have any new suits for the dance-a-thon," Dusty suggested, picking up the pace.

"Oh? Do we have to dress up? If that's the case, I'll wear one of the suits I already own. I don't want to spend my allowance on a new suit," Marvin said, lagging behind.

Dusty turned around, "Come on, Marvin. It's for a good cause. Plus, those suits are old, and we have to look sharp if we want to win the dance-a-thon! I'm sure we can find a new outfit that will match better with that bright green bow tie you always like to wear," Dusty teased.

Marvin chuckled, "Hey! I like my green bow tie. It looks good with my grey fur! All right, I guess it wouldn't hurt to look. But I'd rather do more sleuthing to figure out who the Geomath Landscaping cats are. It's still puzzling me a lot."

"I know you want to investigate. I'm curious too. Let's go get new suits, and then maybe later we can do some more investigating," Dusty stalled, attempting to veer Marvin off the scent that he was hiding something.

"Okay," Marvin agreed.

"So, do you have anyone in mind yet to be your dance partner?" Dusty asked.

Marvin laughed, "Haha, maybe. I think you know."

"Keisha? The grey tabby cat who always wears a pink bow on her head?" Dusty guessed.

"Yes, she's a great dancer and might help me not trip over myself!" Marvin explained.

"I think that's great!" Dusty exclaimed, relieved that Marvin was now focused on finding a dance partner for the dance-a-thon and not on uncovering the mystery of the Geomath Landscaping Company.

"How much further?" Marvin asked, panting.

"Right this way!" Dusty exclaimed as he led Marvin toward the Suit Yourself clothing store.

As they walked into the store, Marvin and Dusty were greeted by rows of colorful suits and ties. They spent some time browsing the racks and trying different outfits but eventually made their selections and checked out at the counter.

WITH THEIR NEW SUITS in hand, Marvin and Dusty stepped out of the store and into the bright sunshine. The fresh spring air filled their lungs as they walked down the street, feeling proud of their purchases.

"This was a great idea! I can't wait to wear my new suit!" Marvin exclaimed.

"Yes, you're going to look dashing! When will you ask Keisha if she'll be your dance partner?" Dusty inquired.

"I think I'll ask her tomorrow. I hope she'll say yes!"

"Oh, I think she will. She's one of the best dancers in our class," Dusty said with a smile.

Marvin nodded in agreement. "Remember how she won last year's dance-a-thon with Spike? They danced for hours!"

Dusty chuckled. "Yeah, Spike was so exhausted he was late for school every day for a week afterward."

Marvin laughed. "I hope I can keep up with her! I'm not the best dancer."

Dusty patted him on the back. "You're too modest. You'll do great, especially with Keisha by your side, and who knows, maybe you'll even win the grand prize this year!"

Marvin's eyes lit up. "That would be amazing. I'll just need to keep my energy up and dance as long as I can. Anyways, now that we have our suits, why don't we look around town to see what else the Geomath Landscaping Company has been up to?"

"Well, I'm a bit tired now after all this shopping. Can we do some investigating another day?" Dusty stalled.

"Sure, I guess it's getting late. We better hurry home," Marvin said.

"Sounds good!" Dusty said with relief.

The two kittens headed back home. Once Dusty was back in his room, he excitedly unlocked his smartphone and opened the Math Quest application, which now displayed the location of the second clue.

He studied the map and zoomed in. The second grey Question Mark icon was located at his school: Alley Cat Middle School. Unfortunately, he would have to wait until Monday to investigate, which couldn't come soon enough because he was anxious to finish the quest and show Marvin what he had been up to, as long as whoever was behind this would allow it.

After what seemed like an endless long weekend, Monday morning finally arrived. Usually, Dusty had to drag himself out of bed at the beginning of the school week, but today was different. He practically bounced out of bed, went through his usual morning routine, and walked to school with Marvin. Once they arrived at their homeroom classroom, Dusty took out his phone and discreetly tried to figure out exactly where the Question Mark icon was positioned on the map.

"What are you looking at so intently on your phone?" Marvin asked as he sat down at his desk.

"Oh, nothing, I...I'm having trouble reading something," Dusty replied nervously.

Dusty realized he must be more careful around Marvin during this quest. He decided to excuse himself to the litter box room to look at his phone in private. Once inside one of the stalls, he looked at the Math Quest app and zoomed in on the map. He noticed the icon was positioned over the school library. *Awesome!* he thought. *That's where I'll go at lunchtime*. But then he realized this would be difficult to do with Marvin around. It's too bad the quest rules were so strict, as he would like to involve his best friend. However, his cat senses were still telling him to trust the process. *Maybe lunchtime is when Marvin should ask Keisha to be his dance partner*, he thought as he started formulating a plan.

Marvin greeted Dusty with a sideways grin as he returned to his desk. "Took you long enough," he teased.

Dusty chuckled. "Hey, when are you asking Keisha to be your dance partner for the dance-a-thon?"

Marvin shrugged as he tried to concentrate on the fraction worksheet that Mrs. Catnip had placed on his desk. "I'm not sure. Maybe at recess or lunch?"

Dusty nodded in agreement. "I think lunchtime would be best. Then you'd have time to strategize with her how you'll win the competition. Plus, I don't mind if you want to eat with her."

Marvin raised an eyebrow. "Really? Are you sure?"

Dusty nodded. "Yeah, go for it! You don't need me tagging along. I should probably scope out a dance partner for myself, too," Dusty said. The minute he uttered the words, he realized this was true. *Wowee,* he thought, *I'm going to be busy!*

"Okay, I'll ask Keisha about the dance-a-thon at lunch. What if she says no, though?" Marvin worried.

"You'll be fine; she won't reject a regal, grey cat like you with a bright green bow tie!" Dusty reassured him.

Marvin turned his attention back to the fraction worksheet before him. "I think we better finish up this assignment," he said.

"Yes, I need to improve my math skills!" Dusty said with an underlying reason in his mind.

The two kittens worked through their math worksheet, attended their other morning classes, and walked to the cafeteria for lunch. They stood at the entrance, scoping out the landscape. The air was filled with excitement, playfulness, and a hint of mischief, and the sound of paws scampering and playful meows filled the room. Some kittens were sharing treats with their friends, while others were showing off their latest toys.

"Where is she?" Dusty said.

"I don't know. I don't see her yet," Marvin replied as he scanned the room for Keisha.

"Well, let's grab our food, and maybe we'll see her. If you want, I can start eating with you, and then I'll disappear so you can have some time to chat."

"Sure, that sounds like a plan," Marvin said.

Marvin and Dusty chose Tuna Florentine for lunch and salmon-flavored treats for dessert. They looked around for Keisha and spotted her sitting at a table toward the back of the room with two other cats: a pure white short-haired cat and a blueish-grey Russian Blue cat. Keisha's tabby fur pattern was striking, and she wore a pink bow on her head.

"Let's go join her!" Dusty urged.

"Ok, but she's sitting with her friends," Marvin hesitated.

"Well, we can sit at the end of the table since there is room, and then we can start a conversation with her," Dusty suggested.

"Alright," Marvin agreed, feeling shy about the whole thing.

They sat down at the end of the table and began eating their lunch, talking about superficial things while waiting for an opportunity to say something to Keisha. Finally, Dusty saw their chance when Keisha started talking to her friends about what they were learning in Math class.

Dusty tapped Marvin's back with his tail.

"Hey!" Marvin said quietly, glaring at him.

"She's talking about math class. You should talk to her!" Dusty whispered.

Marvin sighed, then turned toward Keisha and tried to make conversation, "Did you find the fraction worksheet hard today?"

"It wasn't too bad, but I didn't understand one of the questions," Keisha said.

"Which one? Maybe I can help?" Marvin said.

"That would be great. It's Marvin, right?"

"Yes, and this is my friend, Dusty," Marvin replied.

"Hi, Keisha," Dusty said, turning to Marvin. "I think I'll get going and let you two talk."

"Okay, see you later, Dusty! Thanks for the advice," Marvin said before turning his attention back to Keisha to see what she needed help with on the fraction worksheet.

Finally, Dusty had some time to continue on his quest. He hurried to the library and took out his phone to check if he could find the location where the map icon would become active and reveal the next question.

As he strolled past each row of bookcases, he wondered who could be behind the creation of this quest and why it was a secret. Suddenly, the icon changed from grey to bright red, indicating it was clickable!

He had just passed by the section on astronomy and space science books. *There must be a connection*, he thought, as he moved his paw over the icon and clicked to open the third question.

Problem #3:
The Moon has much less mass than Purrth, so objects on the Moon weigh less than they do on Purrth. A catronaut travels from Purrth to the Moon. On Purrth, he weighs 12 pounds, but on the Moon, he weighs only 2 pounds. The unit for pounds is written *lbs*.

a. If a kitten weighs 2 lbs on Purrth, how much would she weigh on the Moon? Please write your answer as a fraction in its lowest terms.

b. How much would the same kitten weigh on Jupipurr if the ratio between the weight of an object on Purrth to that on Jupipurr is 1: 2.34?

Dusty's eyes veered toward the clock in the upper right corner of his phone. He still had time before lunch was over to solve this problem. He found some scrap paper and sat down at one of the tables in the library to work out the solution.

Okay, objects weigh less on the Moon because it has less gravity than Purrth. The cat who travels to the Moon weighs 12 pounds on Purrth and only 2 pounds on the Moon. The first question asks me to figure out how much a kitten will weigh on the Moon if she weighs 2 pounds on Purrth. This looks like an equivalent ratio problem!

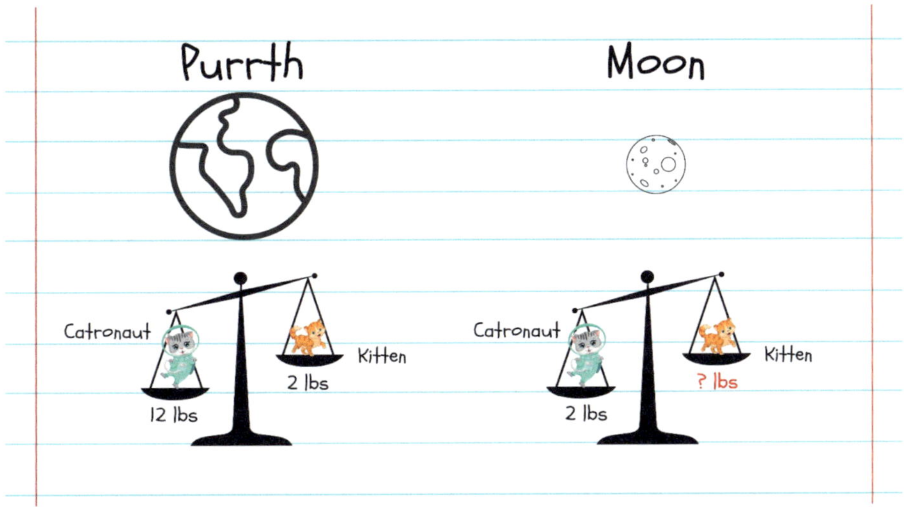

Dusty drew a diagram on his paper to help figure out the ratio between the weight of an object on Purrth and the Moon: *If the catronaut weighs 12 pounds on Purrth and only 2 pounds on the Moon, then the ratio is 12 to 2 or 6 to 1 because you can divide by 2 on both sides of the ratio to get it in its lowest terms.*

$$\div 2 \quad 12 : 2 \quad \div 2$$
$$6 : 1$$

I think this means that an object weighs one-sixth of its weight on the moon compared to its weight on Purrth. So, the ratio must stay the same when comparing a kitten's weight on Purrth to that of the Moon. Therefore, I think I have to divide the kitten's weight on Purrth (2 lbs) by 6 to get the answer! Now, what is 2 divided by 6? Hmmm... Oh, wait, that is a fraction I can break down into its lowest terms.

All I have to do is divide the fraction's numerator and denominator by 2 to get ⅓ because 2 divides evenly into both 2 and 6. So, the answer must be that the kitten would weigh one-third of a pound on the Moon!

$$\frac{2 \div 2}{6 \div 2} = \frac{1}{3} lbs$$

Dusty drew a second diagram on his scrap paper to help him find the answer.

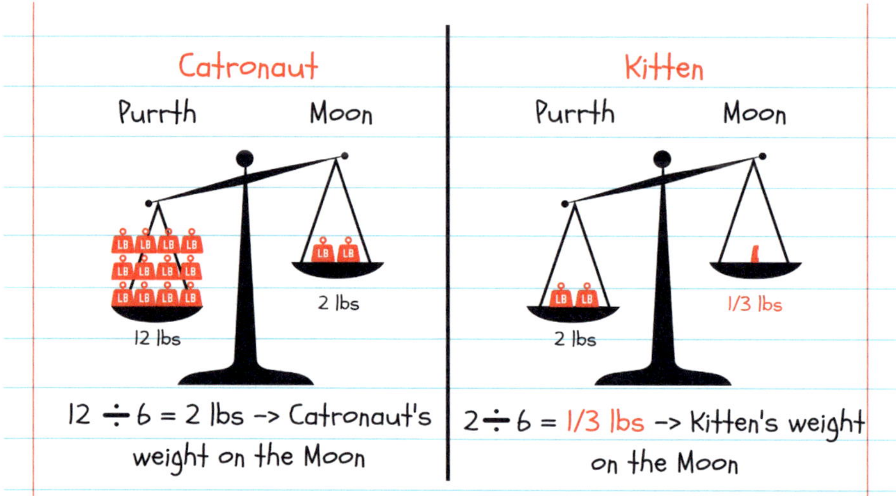

That's interesting how much lighter the kitten would weigh. It would be practically weightless! Well, not really. Dusty chuckled, realizing that was an exaggeration, and checked his steps before proceeding to part b of the question.

Part b looks like a similar problem, so I will have to figure out an equivalent ratio again.

> **b.** How much would the same kitten weigh on Jupipurr if the ratio between the weight of an object on Purrth to that on Jupipurr is 1: 2.34?

Dusty recalled that Jupipurr was the largest planet in the Solar System, so it made sense that objects would weigh much more than on Purrth due to its stronger gravity. *I'll use what we know about the weight of the kitten on Purrth, which is 2 pounds,* he thought. *Since the ratio of an object's weight on Purrth to that of Jupipurr is 1 to 2.34, all I have to do is multiply the weight of the kitten on Purrth (2 lbs) by 2.34, and I'll get the weight of the kitten on Jupipurr! Let me try it!*

Dusty wrote the calculation on paper and computed the answer using his phone's calculator application.

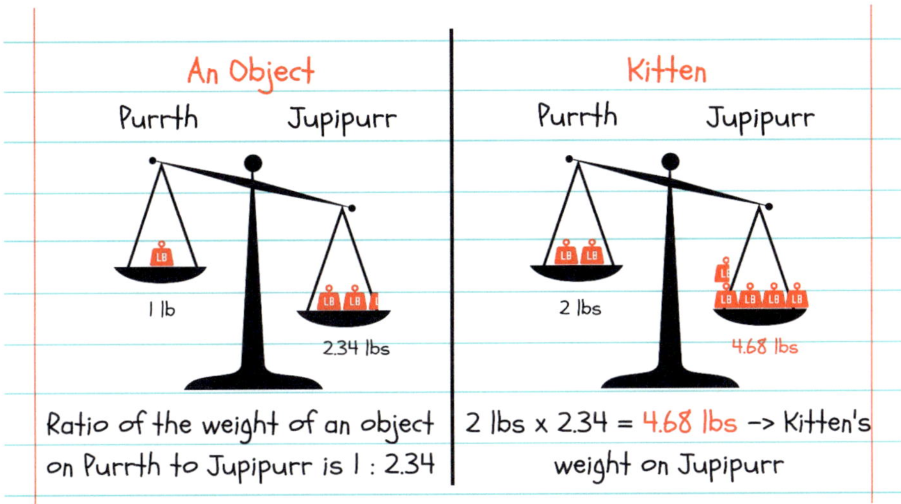

When he was done, he smiled, feeling confident with his calculation. *That makes sense to me! The kitten would weigh 4.68 pounds on Jupipurr, which is 2.34 times more than on Purrth,* he thought.

Dusty confidently entered his answers for both parts of the question into the text boxes provided, his paw hovering over the Submit button. Even though math didn't come as naturally to him as it did to Marvin, he felt he was grasping these real-world applications much better than the math worksheets and tests he did in school. With a deep breath, he closed his eyes and pressed the Submit button. When he opened his eyes again, he saw the word *"Congratulations!"* on the screen.

As Dusty celebrated his victory, his attention was drawn to another grey-colored Question Mark icon that appeared on the map, this time over Cata Monica Beach. Even though Purrfect Paradise was close to a few stunning beaches, Dusty wasn't particularly fond of water. Nevertheless, he relished soaking up the sun's rays and rolling around in the coarse sand grains. *I'll be off to Cata Monica Beach after school,* he thought, then wandered back to try to find Marvin.

"Hey, Dusty!" Marvin yelled as he spotted Dusty hastily leaving school like he was on a mission.

"Hey!"

"Where are you sneaking off to?" Marvin asked.

"I'm not sneaking!" Dusty replied.

"It looks like you're heading for the bus stop," Marvin observed.

"Well, yes, I am," Dusty replied cryptically.

"Oh, okay, I thought we would hang out after school," Marvin said with disappointment. "Guess what? I asked Keisha if she'd like to be my dance partner at the dance-a-thon, and she said yes! Did you have any luck figuring out who could be your dance partner?"

"That's great! I'm happy for you. No, I forgot about the dance-a-thon and must do something first. Can we meet up later?"

"Sure, no problem," Marvin said, although he was becoming increasingly suspicious of what Dusty was up to.

"I know you're curious about where I'm going, but just trust me. I'll let you know when I can," Dusty reassured.

"Oh, so you *are* up to something!" Marvin exclaimed.

"Well, it's nothing too important, I don't think. Just something I have to do," Dusty said.

"Okay, I get it. I just felt like you had a new best friend, maybe a girlfriend or something!" Marvin said with a wink.

"Hahaha...no, no girlfriend, and you're my only best friend, and that will never change!" Dusty said with a smile.

"Great! I'll catch up with you later. Have fun!"

"Thanks, Marvin."

Marvin and Dusty parted ways, and Dusty waited for the bus impatiently. Finally, the bus arrived and screeched to a stop.

"That will be one dollar," the bus driver said as Dusty entered.

Dusty dropped a few coins through the slot.

"Thank you!" the driver said.

"You're welcome," Dusty said.

Dusty stared intently at the map on his phone as the bus drove past the beaches along the shore. He had to make sure he got off at the right stop, or he would have a long walk ahead of him. As they approached Cata Monica Beach, the icon's location became more precise. Dusty pulled on one of the wires strung along the sides of the bus to signal that he wanted to get off at the next stop. *This should be close enough*, he thought.

The bus came to an abrupt stop, and Dusty bounded out of the vehicle. He walked to Cata Monica Beach, following the icon's lead. He wandered around in the hot sand as the waves lapped on the shore. He only hoped he wouldn't have to get into the water to trigger the next question.

It was a long coastline to cover on foot. Dusty assumed he needed to look for landmarks since the other icons became active near specific items. But this was a beach! He only saw a few cats basking in the sun on the scorching white sand, a couple of lifeguards, and a few brave souls who decided to cool off in the water. Nothing else!

How was he going to find the exact spot to activate the icon? He stopped and scanned the distance with his excellent eyesight. No, he couldn't see anything of note. *Maybe he was in the wrong area*, he thought.

As he dragged his paws through the soft sand, he focused on the Math Quest app and nearly tripped over a spherical rock. He stumbled, glancing at the map on his phone, and noticed the icon had just turned red!

He stopped abruptly and hastily pressed the question mark icon to reveal the following question:

Problem #4:

When planets are seen close together in the night sky, their formation is called a **conjunction**. In a simple solar system, three planets, A, B, and C, revolve around their star, as depicted in the diagram, starting in a lined-up configuration with their star. If planet A takes 1 year to complete one revolution, planet B takes 2 years to complete one revolution, and planet C takes 4 years to complete one revolution, answer the following questions:

a. After how many years will planets A and B line up in conjunction?

b. When will all three planets come into conjunction?

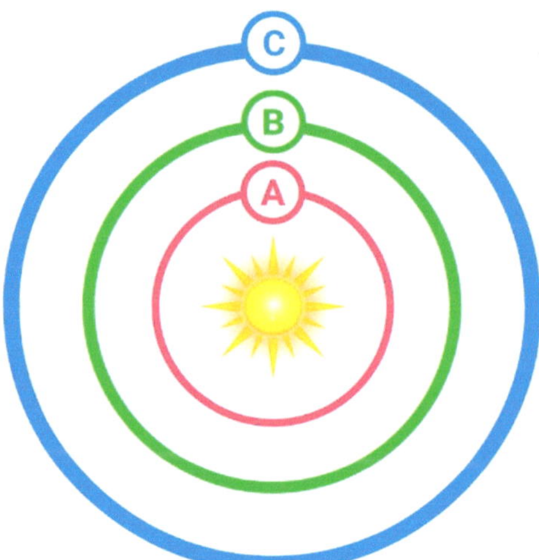

This one was going to be fun! he thought. Dusty had always enjoyed problems where he could draw a diagram to figure out a solution. He began to look around and realized that he could use the sand on the beach to sketch a diagram of the three planets in orbit around their star. As he looked closer at the spot where he had almost tripped, he noticed two other spherical rocks lying about and a stick, half buried in the fine, loose sand grains. It was almost like these objects had been left in the sand for him to use. *How convenient*, he thought, *yet how mysterious*.

Dusty continued to contemplate: *So, we know the time for each planet to revolve around its star. I should be able to draw this in the sand to determine when they will line up again.*

Using the stick, Dusty drew a diagram in the sand, similar to the diagram on his phone screen. He decided to use the three spherical rocks as the planets and located a sand dollar that he planned to use for the star in the middle.

Dusty pushed the rocks around in the sand using the stick to simulate them revolving around their star. *Planet A will revolve around its Sun in one year,* he thought. *At that point, planet B will be only halfway around its orbit. Then, after two years, planet A will have made a second revolution around the star, and planet B will have completed one revolution. So, they will line up again in two years!*

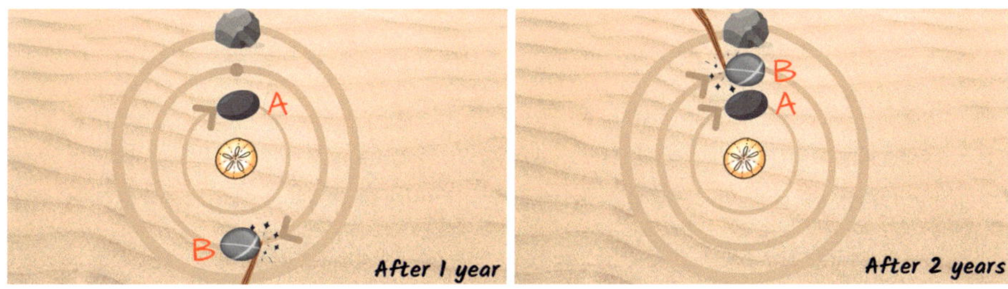

He then worked out the second part of the question in the sand.

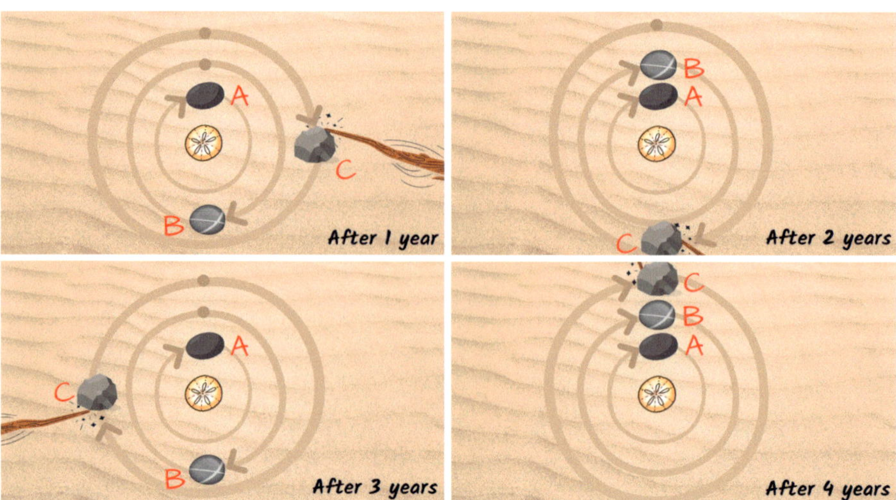

For question b, I have to think about the third planet taking four years to revolve around its star. That would mean planet A would make four revolutions in four years, planet B would make two revolutions in four years, and planet C would make one revolution in four years. This means that all three planets would line up again after planet C makes one revolution. I wonder what math concept this is since I've only been using common sense so far to find the solution.

Suddenly, he remembered something from math class. *Maybe I need to look for the Least Common Multiple or LCM between the three revolution periods?* He decided to find the LCM to see if it would work the same way to determine when all three planets would line up. He took out his phone, opened a drawing app, and typed out all the multiples for each revolution period in a table format and then shaded in the lowest number between the three sets:

Planet A	1	2	3	4	5	6...
Planet B	2	4	6	8	10	12...
Planet C	4	8	12	16	20	24...

Planet A would have revolution periods of 1 year, 2 years, 3 years, and so on since it takes one year to complete one revolution. Planet B would have revolution periods of 2 years, 4 years, 6 years, and so on since it takes 2 years to complete one revolution. Planet C would have revolution periods of 4 years, 8 years, 12 years, and so on since it takes 4 years to complete one revolution. It looks like 4 is the lowest number they all have in common. Therefore, the LCM must be 4 years. Wow! It's the same! I must be right then, Dusty thought. He typed his responses to the two questions and clicked Submit. He was confident he had done this one correctly, and he had. The next Question Mark icon appeared on the map, so Dusty zoomed in with his paw to look closer at the location. Oh, my, it seemed like it was positioned on top of Marvin's house!

This is going to be interesting, Dusty thought. *How will I snoop around Marvin's house until the icon becomes active to access the fifth problem? Plus, how many more questions are there? I'm not sure I can continue in secret much longer.*

One good thing was that he hadn't been gone too long. He glanced at his phone and realized it was just about supper time. After supper, he planned to text Marvin to see if he could hang out at his house. This would allow him to figure out the answer to the next math problem.

AFTER SUPPER, DUSTY TEXTED Marvin:

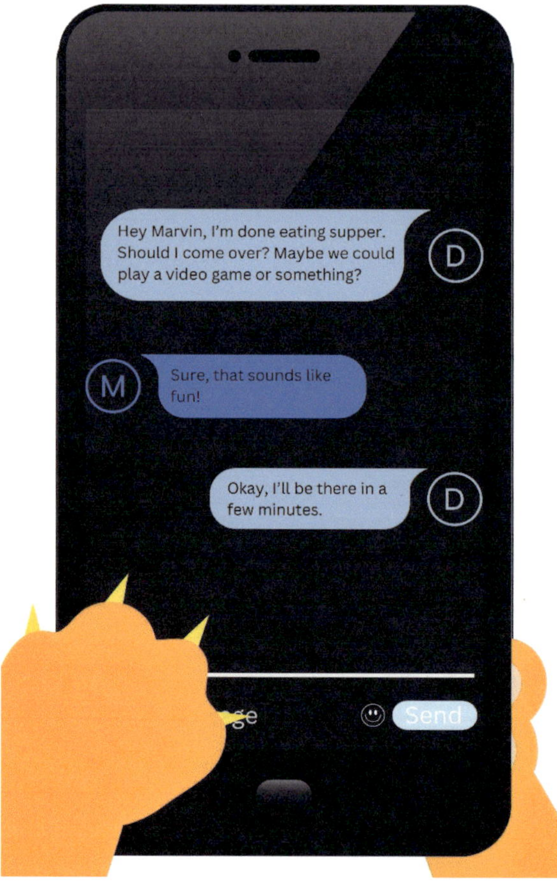

Minutes later, Dusty tapped on Marvin's front door with his claws.

"Hi, come on in! What video game do you want to play?" Marvin asked as he let Dusty into his house.

"Umm...I don't know. Let me look at your collection again," Dusty said as he thought about how he would tour through Marvin's house without him wondering why.

"Okay, come upstairs, and we'll take a look," Marvin said.

The kittens scampered upstairs. Dusty kept his phone handy to glance at the map in the Math Quest application. Nope, the Question Mark icon was not active yet.

As he pawed through Marvin's extensive collection of video games, Dusty felt overwhelmed. He was eager to uncover the next math problem but didn't want to reveal his actions to Marvin just yet. Trying to focus on the task at hand, he recognized some of his favorite video games in Marvin's collection, like "Super Mario Kitten" and "Pawblox," but there were also many he had never heard of. He found himself reading the game titles almost absent-mindedly, his mind wandering about how to find the next clue.

"So, which one?" Marvin asked impatiently.

"Umm...just a minute, I have to look through them all. You have so many I can never remember what you have," Dusty replied.

"How about this one?" Marvin suggested as he pointed.

"Nahhh. You know, I think I've changed my mind. I'm not sure I want to play now. I'll...I'll be right back," Dusty said as he hurried out of the room toward the litter box. Marvin stood frozen in disbelief.

Dusty held his phone up in front of his face as he ran down the hallway. He deliberately passed by the litter box room to quickly check the other rooms on the top floor first. Nothing. He then reversed his steps and walked back to the litter box room, which was small but cozy, with a window that let in just enough natural light. He stared at himself in the mirror. What was he going to do?

"Hey Marvin, I'm thirsty, so I'm going to grab a bone broth soda from the kitchen," Dusty yelled as he walked downstairs.

"Okay," Marvin said, "I'm just browsing the news online."

Marvin's parents lounged in the backyard, making it easier for Dusty to snoop around their house unnoticed. He wandered into the kitchen, opened the refrigerator door, and pretended to grab a soda. Then he continued walking downstairs, closely monitoring the Question Mark icon on the map.

As he moved through the living room, dining room, and another litter box room, the app showed no change. But when he entered the study, designed as a cozy reading nook with rows of books lining the wall, his cat senses tingled, and his fur raised on the back of his neck. He glanced at his phone and saw that the icon had turned red! Finally, the icon was active. *Which books triggered it this time?*

Dusty clicked the red Question Mark icon, and another clue appeared as a short poem instead of a math problem. He assumed this was because he was almost at the end of the math quest. Hooray!

A secret place lies within,
But only a friend can let you in,
You may now reveal your quest,
So that you can finish this test!

Can I finally tell Marvin what I've been working on? Dusty thought. He concluded that this was what the clue meant and bounded upstairs with an excitement he hadn't felt in a while.

"Marvin! Marvin!" Dusty panted.

"What? What's wrong?"

"Nothing, nothing," Dusty said as he tried to catch his breath. "I'm just happy because I can finally tell you about something."

"Okay," Marvin said with curiosity and hesitation.

"I've been working on a secret math quest that appeared on my phone the other day. I think it was sent to me by the Geomath Landscaping cats, or at least that's my hunch. The instructions said I couldn't tell anyone about it, so I've been sneaking around trying to solve math problems without you finding out. But finally, I'm allowed to tell you because I think I need something you know about to solve the last math problem," Dusty explained quickly.

"Wow, that's crazy! I knew something was going on, but I would never have guessed this," Marvin laughed. "How did you do on the math problems so far?"

"Well, I've been getting them all correct," Dusty said proudly. "I guess some of your math expertise has been rubbing off on me!"

"It's been hard not to bug you about what you've been up to, but I managed to distract myself. I guess getting ready for the spring dance-a-thon has helped," Marvin said.

"So anyway," Dusty continued, "the last problem seems to involve something in your study. The last math problem won't appear until we figure out what that is."

Dusty showed Marvin the map on the phone and the clue that appeared when he was in the study.

Marvin peered over his shoulder, “ICAP Math Quest...what does that mean?”

“I don’t know, but maybe we’ll find out soon?” Dusty replied. “Is there anything in the study that may trigger the last problem to appear?”

“Well, there’s a secret room adjoining the study,” Marvin said, “but how would anyone know about that? This is a bit odd.”

“I know it’s strange, but my cat senses have been telling me to trust the process. So, where’s this secret room? How do we open it?”

“Well, I’ve never been in there myself, but I know there’s a secret lever or button in the study that opens it. We’ll have to do some hunting around.”

“Okay, sounds good. Let’s go!” Dusty exclaimed.

“Hold on. I’m not sure I’m allowed in there,” Marvin said as he paused, “but as long as we don’t disturb anything, it should be fine, I hope.”

“If our hunch is correct, the only way for me to finish this quest is for us to go into that room,” Dusty explained. “This is probably a good time to do it since your parents are on the patio.”

“Okay, okay. Let’s go check it out.”

The two kittens quietly ran downstairs to the study. Dusty sniffed and searched around for anything unusual. "I don't see anything that might lead to a secret room from here," Dusty said.

"I know, but it could look completely normal. It could be a book, a book stand, or maybe that stool in the corner of the room. Just use your paws and gently touch things as you sniff around. Maybe there is a button somewhere," Marvin suggested.

Marvin moved over to the desk at the back of the room and began to open each drawer, one at a time. He used his paws to feel inside each one but found nothing. As Marvin peered underneath the desk and moved his paws over the wood surface, he felt something like a soft cat treat. "Hey Dusty, I think I may have found something."

"What is it?" Dusty asked as he ran over to join Marvin.

"Look under here," Marvin said as he pointed under the desk.

"Hey! It looks like a button!" Dusty exclaimed.

"Yes. I'll push it since it's my house, just in case we get in trouble," Marvin said.

Marvin pushed the so-called button, but nothing happened. Unfazed, he tried again and then a third time, holding it down for a few seconds. Suddenly, they heard a click and watched in amazement as one of the bookcases along the far wall slid toward the left, as though it were on rails, to reveal a tiny door on the opposite side of the room.

"Look! There's a door!" Dusty exclaimed.

They ran over to it but hesitated to enter. Noticing that Dusty needed some guidance, Marvin gestured for Dusty to stand behind him as he slowly turned the knob and tip-toed into the secret room. Dusty followed closely behind, intrigued by the mysterious space they had just discovered. Glancing at his phone, Dusty noticed that the last math problem had just appeared; however, at that moment, he was more captivated by the mysterious space before them.

The room was covered in cobwebs, which Marvin happily munched on as they were one of his favorite treats — like cotton candy for cats!

He led the way, using the light on his phone to guide them through the small space. A creaky antique brown desk and a small wooden chair stood in the far corner. The desk's surface was scattered with yellowed paper, dusty old books, and an antique lamp that appeared to have long stopped working. Directly across from the desk was a large safe bolted tightly to the wall.

"What's this room used for?" Dusty asked as he looked around at the dreary surroundings.

"I'm not exactly sure," Marvin said, "but judging by the safe, I would say it's where some important information is kept or where my parents hid some money! It doesn't seem like they've been in this room for a long time, though, since there are so many cobwebs. What are these strange, old books?"

"I don't know, very strange," Dusty repeated as he opened one of the books and began to paw through it. It seemed to be written in a bizarre language he had never seen before.

"So, what are we supposed to do in here? Does the app tell you yet?" Marvin asked.

"Yes, the last problem appeared when we walked into the room. Here it is," Dusty said as he showed Marvin his phone.

Problem #5:

A friendly alien cat species visits Purrth to deliver a message. Below are the clues to what it says. Use your math skills to decipher the message. Each answer corresponds to a letter shown in brackets at the end of each question. Write the letter corresponding to each answer on the blank lines below to reveal the secret message!

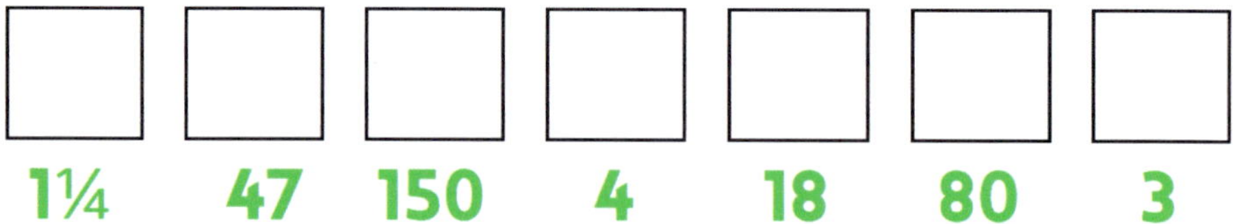

a. 15% of 120 = ____ **(P)**

b. If you have 15 quarters, how many whole dollars do you have? **(A)**

c. If you have half a pizza and your friend has three-quarters of a pizza, how much pizza do you have in total? Please write your answer as a fraction in its lowest terms. **(C)**

d. If Flash the Cat can run 60 miles in 2 hours, how far can he run in 5 hours? **(T)**

e. How many questions did Buffy get correct out of 50 if she received a mark of 94% on her math test? **(A)**

f. 80 is 100% of what number? **(I)**

g. 15 ÷ (5 – 2) – 1 = ____ **(O)**

"This looks like fun!" Marvin said.

"Yes, I like to figure out secret messages," Dusty replied.

a. 15% of 120 = ____ (P)

"Okay, let's work through the problems together. So, the first one is 15% of 120. Hmm...maybe we can do this one in our heads."

"Really? How can we do that? I would be using my calculator," Dusty replied.

"Well, we could find out what 10% of 120 is and then divide that in half to find out what 5% of 120 is and then add the two numbers, which should give us 15% of 120," Marvin explained.

"That sounds complicated, but ok," Dusty said, feeling overwhelmed with having to estimate this in his head.

"First of all, what's 10% of 120?" Marvin asked.

"I don't know," Dusty admitted.

"What does percent mean?" Marvin prompted.

"Oh, I know this! It means per one hundred and can be written as a fraction over 100."

"Yes! So, 10% means 10 out of 100. Let me write this down on the back of one of these pieces of paper," Marvin said as he searched for a writing tool.

"There's a pencil," Dusty noticed, pointing to one on the floor.

"Great, thank you! Okay, let's write this down." Marvin wrote on the piece of paper:

$$15\%\ of\ 120 = ?$$

$$10\% = \frac{10}{100}\frac{\div 10}{\div 10}$$

$$10\% = \frac{1}{10}$$

"Does this make sense?" Marvin asked.

"Yes, I think so," Dusty replied.

Marvin continued to explain, "We have 10 over 100, which is the same as 1 over 10 or one-tenth because you can divide by 10 in both the numerator and denominator of the fraction to reduce it to its lowest form. 10 divided by 10 in the numerator equals 1, and 100 divided by 10 in the denominator equals 10."

"Yes, I see that. You're reducing the fraction to its lowest form," Dusty repeated.

"There are ten 12's in the number 120 because 10 multiplied by 12 equals 120. So, this means 10% or one-tenth of 120 equals 12," Marvin continued.

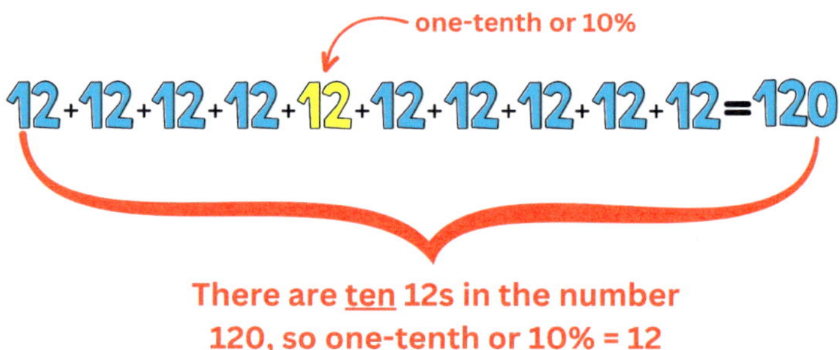

"Oh, I get it. So, if I have a bag of 10 candies and I eat one candy, I ate one-tenth of the bag of candy?" Dusty asked.

"Exactly! Wow, you're really getting good at math!" Marvin exclaimed, impressed by Dusty's skills.

"Thanks, this math quest has been a big help to my self-confidence with solving math problems," Dusty replied.

"Getting back to the problem, one-tenth means dividing by 10. One way to check our answer is to move the decimal point over to the left one place value. When you move the decimal point over to the left, you're dividing the number by 10. So, if you start with 120 and move the decimal point over one spot, you get 12. 10% of 120 equals 12. Now, to find 5%, we need to divide 10% by 2," Marvin continued.

Move the decimal point over once to the left to determine one-tenth or 10% of any number!

"Right, that makes sense. So, if 10% of 120 is 12, then 5% of 120 would be half of that, which is 6," Dusty concluded.

one-tenth or 10%

12+12+12+12+12+12+12+12+12+12=120

6 6

If 10% of 120 = 12
Then 5% of 120 = 6

"Great job! Now, all we have to do is add 10% and 5% to get 15%. So, 15% of 120 equals 12 plus 6, which is 18. Does that answer match one of the blanks in the secret message?" Marvin asked.

$$\begin{aligned}15\%\ of\ 120 &= (10\%\ of\ 120) + (5\%\ of\ 120)\\ &= 12 + 6\\ &= \mathbf{18}\end{aligned}$$

"Yes, it does, and since each answer corresponds to a specific letter, all we have to do is type that letter on the blank above each answer. In this case, it's the letter 'P,'" Dusty replied.

"That's right!" Marvin said as he took the phone from Dusty's paws and typed 'P' on the blank line above the answer.

"Hey!" Dusty exclaimed, slightly annoyed that Marvin had taken his phone.

Dusty grabbed his phone back and said, "Okay, the next problem is about quarters. It says, 'If you have 15 quarters, how many whole dollars do you have?'"

b. If you have 15 quarters, how many whole dollars do you have? (A)

"This one is pretty easy, I think," Marvin said confidently.

"Yes, I think I know it already. There are 4 quarters in a dollar, so how many groups of *4 quarters* are in the number 15? Well, that would be 3 because 3 times 4 is 12. Therefore, you would have 3 whole dollars. Plus, you would have 3 quarters left over."

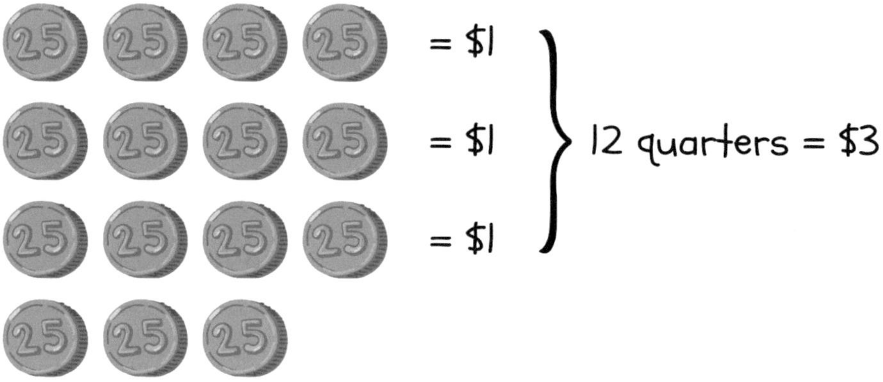

"That's exactly what I was thinking too! What letter is beside the answer?" Marvin asked as he looked at Dusty's phone.

"It's the letter 'A,'" Dusty replied as he typed 'A' on the blank line above the 3 in the secret message.

The two kittens continued working through the problems, and Marvin's scrap paper filled up with math symbols and equations. One by one, they solved each question and started seeing the secret message emerge.

c. If you have half a pizza and your friend has three-quarters of a pizza, how much pizza do you have

in total? Please write your answer as a fraction in its lowest terms. (C)

"Yummm, pizza, now I'm hungry," Dusty said as he licked his chops.

"Haha, yes, this question makes me hungry too. So, if I have half a pizza and you have three-quarters of a pizza, then we would have the following result," Marvin said as he drew pictures of pizza on the piece of paper.

$$\frac{1}{2} + \frac{3}{4} = 1 \quad \frac{1}{4}$$

"This one is easy to visualize when you draw pictures. Half a pizza plus three-quarters equals one whole pizza plus one-quarter of another," Dusty explained.

"Yes, that's right. Therefore, we would have one and one-quarter pieces of pizza. Here's another way to figure it out using fractions," Marvin said as he wrote down the fraction equivalents on the paper.

$$\frac{1}{2} + \frac{3}{4} = ?$$

"Oh, I see. We are adding fractions, so we have to find a common denominator to add these together. If we multiply one half by 2 on the top and bottom of the fraction, then we would have 4 as the common denominator," Dusty said.

"Exactly!" Marvin exclaimed as he wrote down what Dusty said.

$$\frac{1 \times 2}{2 \times 2} + \frac{3}{4} = ?$$

$$\frac{2}{4} + \frac{3}{4} = \frac{5}{4}$$

$$= \mathbf{1\frac{1}{4}}$$

"Yup, the answer matches what we figured out with the pizza pictures. So, we would have one whole pizza plus one-quarter of another pizza, equaling 1¼," Marvin said.

"Good, the answer is there, so we can write a 'C' on the blank."

At this point, Marvin and Dusty stared at the secret message to see if they could guess what it might spell out from the answers they had found up to now. But they couldn't determine what the message was yet.

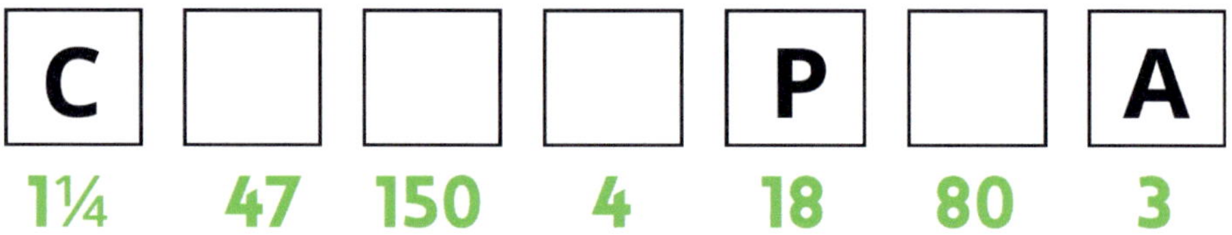

"Onto the next question!" Marvin said.

d. If Flash the Cat can run 60 miles in 2 hours, how far can he run in 5 hours? (T)

"So, would we set up a proportion?" Dusty asked.

"Yes, that's right—like this," Marvin said as he wrote down the equation.

$$\frac{60\ miles}{2\ hours} = \frac{?\ miles}{5\ hours}$$

"If Flash the Cat runs 60 miles in 2 hours, wouldn't he run 30 miles in one hour?" Dusty asked.

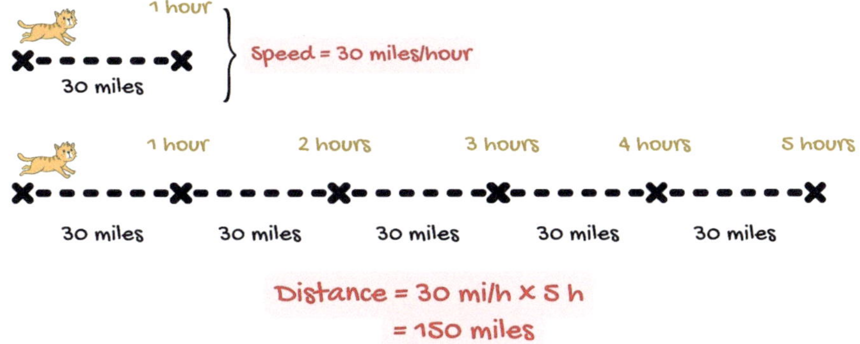

"Excellent observation, Dusty! By finding out how fast he runs in one hour, we can multiply that by 5 to determine how far he runs in 5 hours. Let me see, 30 multiplied by 5 would be 150 because 3 x 5 = 15, then multiply that by 10 to get 150."

$$\frac{60\ miles}{2\ hours} = 30\ miles/hour$$

$$\rightarrow 30\ miles/hour\ \times 5\ \text{hours}$$

$$\boldsymbol{Distance = 150\ miles}$$

"You're quick with the mental math, Marvin!" Dusty complimented.

"Thanks! So, we have 150 miles as the distance that Flash the Cat can travel in 5 hours. The letter corresponding to this answer is 'T.' We're getting closer!" Marvin said.

"Ok, let's hurry. We don't want your parents to catch us in this secret room!"

"I suppose we could leave and solve these problems elsewhere, but we don't know if they will still be available outside this room," Marvin said.

"You might be right. Let's continue."

e. How many questions did Buffy get correct out of 50 if she received a mark of 94% on her math test? (A)

"Okay, we have another proportion to solve. This time, we want to find out how many questions she got correct out of 50 if she received a mark of 94% on her math test. I'll write it down to help us figure it out," Marvin said, locating another piece of paper from the pile on the desk. "On the left side of the equation, we have the number of questions she got correct, represented by a question mark, and on the right side, we have her score as a percentage," Marvin said as he wrote:

$$\frac{?}{50} = 94\%$$

"Oh, and 94% is the same as 94 over 100, so we can re-write that," Dusty said.

"Correct," Marvin said as he replaced the percentage with a fraction:

$$\frac{?}{50} = \frac{94}{100}$$

"I think I did a problem like this earlier in the math quest," Dusty realized.

"Then this should be easy! Since the fractions are equivalent, we need to determine what to multiply the numerator and denominator by to make them equal," Marvin said.

"Yes, I remember. We need to find a number that multiplies evenly into the numerator and denominator of one fraction to make it equal to the other fraction," Dusty explained.

"Right, so if we divide—"

"If we divide 100 by 2, we get 50 which is the total number of points possible for the test. Then if we divide 94 by 2, we should get the unknown mark out of 50 points," Dusty explained, interrupting Marvin.

"Right. So, we can simplify the equation like this," Marvin said as he wrote:

$$\frac{94 \div 2}{100 \div 2} = \frac{?}{50}$$

"Now, we need to solve for the question mark. Dusty, do you remember how we estimated the answer for the last problem?" Marvin asked.

"Yes, we broke the number down into smaller numbers and did some mental math," Dusty replied.

"Exactly. Let's do the same thing here. We know 94 is close to 100, so the answer should be close to 50. Let's break 94 down into 90 and 4. What's half of 90?" Marvin asked.

$$94 = 90 + 4$$

"Umm...half of 9 is 4.5, so half of 90 would be 45," Dusty said as he thought aloud.

"Good job. Now, what's half of 4?" Marvin asked.

"That would be 2," Dusty replied, gabbing the pencil from Marvin.

"Now, we just add 45 and 2 to get the answer," Marvin said as Dusty solved the problem on paper.

$$94 \div 2 = (90 + 4) \div 2$$

What is half of 90? What is half of 4?

$$= (90 \div 2) + (4 \div 2)$$

Half of 90 = 45, and half of 4 = 2:

$$= 45 + 2$$
$$= \mathbf{47}$$

"So, Buffy got 47 questions correct on her math test," Dusty said as he wrote down the answer.

"Great job! That corresponds to another letter, 'A,'" Marvin said as he typed the letter on the blank line above the answer on Dusty's phone.

"Isn't there a much faster way to figure this out?" Dusty said.

"Yes, actually, there is. All you have to do is—"

"Wait! I think I know it. Since 94% equals 94 divided by 100, you can convert 94% to a decimal by moving the decimal point over two places to the left. So that is 0.94. Then all you have to do is multiply 0.94 by 50 to determine 94% of 50, and you should get 47 as the answer," Dusty explained.

"Very good! That's the easiest way to do it, but it's also good to know how to set up the proportion to understand how it represents two equivalent fractions," Marvin said.

"Agreed. I wonder if we can make any sense of the secret message yet," Dusty said as they looked at his phone.

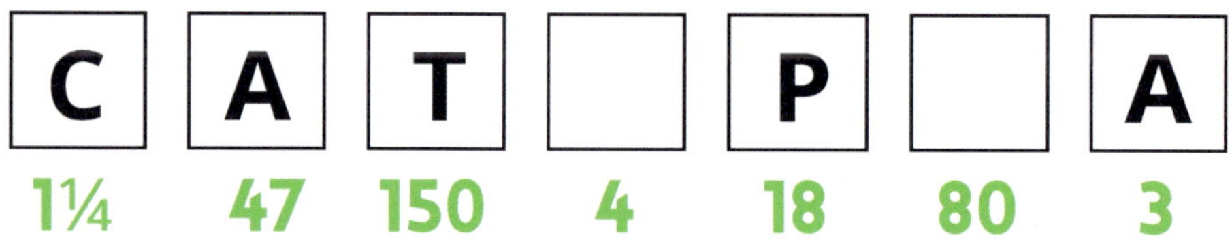

"It looks like CAT something," Dusty said.

"C-A-T-P-A," Marvin spelled out loud. "Hmm, this is a tough one."

"Yeah, I can't think of any words off the top of my head," Dusty said, furrowing his brow.

"Let's think about this logically. What words start with 'cat' and end with a?"

"Caterpillar?" Dusty suggested.

Marvin shook his head. "No, that ends with an 'r,' and it's too long."

Dusty laughed. "I know, I was just joking. Let's keep going, as we only have two more problems!"

f. 80 is 100% of what number? (I)

"80 is 100% of what number? Hmm...this one seems tricky, or at least the wording does. Let's talk it out. Let's first look at the definition of what 100% means," Marvin said as he wrote down the meaning:

$$100\% = \frac{100}{100} = 1$$

"Oh, okay, I sometimes forget 100% just means 1," Dusty said.

"Let's draw a diagram to help us think about this problem. Suppose we bought a jar of candy from the corner store. The label on the jar says there are 80 pieces of candy in it," Marvin explained as he drew a jar and labeled it with "80 pieces" of candy.

100% of the candy
= 80 pieces

"Okay, and?"

"Well, right now, we have all the candy in that jar. We have 100% of it!"

"Yes, right..." Dusty said with a sideways grin.

"Let's suppose you now ate all the candy in the jar," Marvin continued.

"Hey! I'm not always the one who eats all the candy!" Dusty exclaimed.

"I know," Marvin chuckled, "it's just to help us visualize the problem. Now you have eaten 100% of the candy in the jar, which is 80 pieces. So, 80 is 100% of what number? Well, that number is just 80. Does that make sense?"

"Yes, I think so. If you have 100% of the candy in the jar, you have all 80 pieces. If you write a test and there are 80 points possible on the test, and you get 100%, then you get all 80 points. It makes sense but makes you think!"

"That's right! That's a good way to look at it. Always try to think of something simple that is similar. Sometimes it can help you solve the problem. So, I will put the letter 'I' on the blank. I think I know the message now, but let's continue because we are on the last problem!" Marvin said with excitement.

g. 15 ÷ (5 – 2) – 1 = ____ (O)

"Oh, one of these," Dusty groaned.

"Yes, this is the order of operations or BEDMAS," Marvin explained confidently.

"You're right, and **BEDMAS** stands for **B**rackets, **E**xponents, **D**ivision, **M**ultiplication, **A**ddition, **S**ubtraction," Dusty added.

"Yes, so we start by doing the operation in brackets, then—"

"Then we divide, and then we subtract," Dusty interrupted.

"Exactly, let's do it!" Marvin began to write it out on paper.

$$15 \div (5 - 2) - 1 = ?$$
$$15 \div 3 - 1 = ?$$
$$5 - 1 = \mathbf{4}$$

"You know that wasn't half bad!" Dusty said, "I think I'm getting the hang of math better!"

"Excellent! So, the last letter is 'O.' Therefore, the secret message is Ca-to-pi-a...Catopia," Marvin announced as he grabbed Dusty's phone to enter the last letter into its respective blank in the Math Quest app.

"What's Catopia?" Dusty asked rhetorically as he regained possession of his phone from Marvin.

"My thoughts exactly. I'm not sure. It sounds like a place, but nowhere I've ever heard of," Marvin replied.

"Yeah, nothing is coming up when I search on my phone," Dusty added.

"Strange. I think we have all the questions correct, so let's hit the submit button and see if that helps make sense of the word *Catopia*," Marvin suggested.

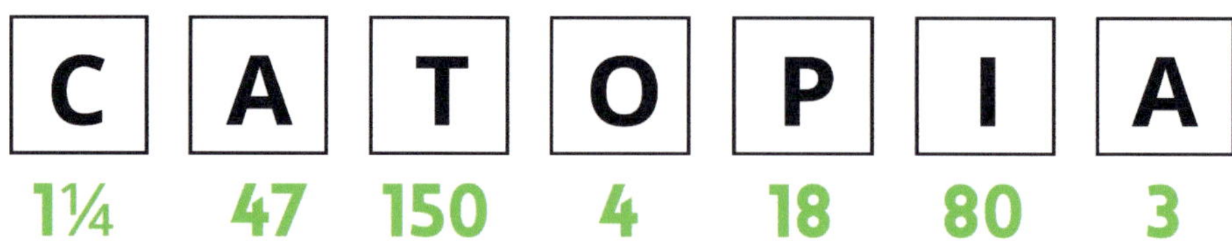

Dusty cautiously pressed the Submit button, and the kittens held their breath as they waited for a response from the Math Quest app.

"We did it!" screamed Dusty as he saw the "Congratulations" notice appear on the screen.

"Great! But not so loud," Marvin said, "my parents might hear us and find out that we opened the secret room."

"Right, right. Sorry," Dusty whispered.

"So, what do we do now?" Marvin asked.

"Well, let's look at the app again. Maybe it will tell us something," Dusty suggested.

The two kittens peered at Dusty's phone. For a moment, they only saw words indicating that the math quest was complete. Then, another notice appeared on the screen:

> *Very well done! You have both made it to the next stage of the process. Thank you for working secretly until the end; we had to be sure you would both be a good fit.*
>
> *All will be revealed very soon, and you will learn more about Catopia. Keep your eyes open for something "blue" in the coming days.*

"Good fit for what?" Marvin asked.

"I don't know, but it sounds like we have another clue—something blue," Dusty said.

"It's exciting but also very odd. Why all the secrecy, I wonder?" Marvin said out loud to himself.

"I know, but for now, all we can do is wait for our next clue to appear and focus on the dance-a-thon, which is coming up very soon. That reminds me, I have to find a dance partner!" Dusty exclaimed quietly.

"Haha...yes, you better! After talking me into asking Keisha!" Marvin teased.

As the two kittens left the secret room, the word "Catopia" echoed in their minds. They had no idea what it meant, but they knew it was important. Marvin couldn't shake off the feeling that something big and mysterious was going on, something involving math and outer space. As they walked back to his room to play video games, the kittens couldn't wait to unravel the secrets of Catopia. Little did they know that their adventure was only beginning and that they would soon embark on a journey that would take them beyond their wildest dreams.

TO BE CONTINUED...

Cat-tivity: Number Sense

COMPLETE THE FOLLOWING MATH problems. Consult the story to help you! The answer key is at the end of the book.

1. It takes the planet Paws approximately 2 years to make one revolution around the Sun. How many years does it take Paws to make four revolutions around the Sun?

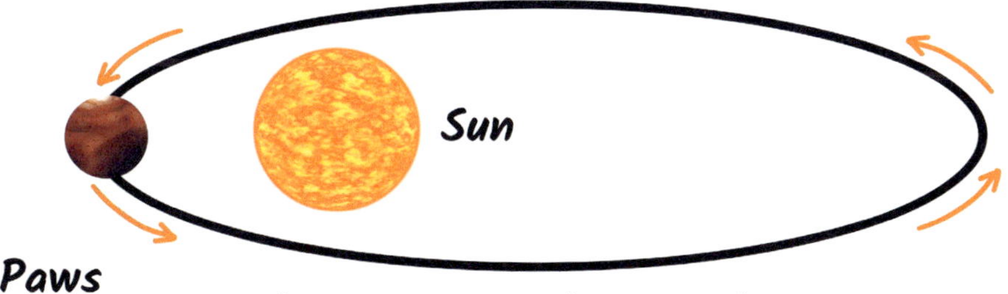

2. Imagine you are on a spaceship traveling from your home planet, Purrth, to the Sun. The distance between Purrth and the Sun is 93,000,000 miles and is called an Astronomical Unit (AU). Astronomical Units are used to measure distances in space.

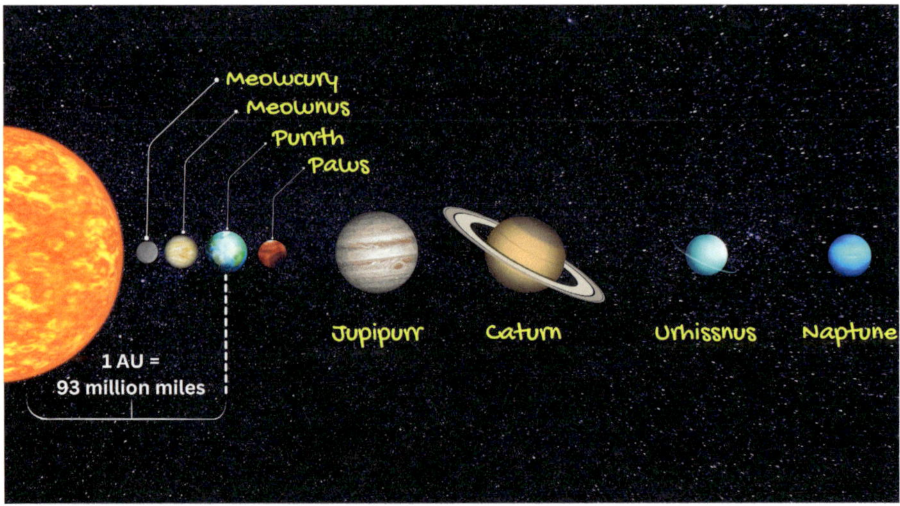

a. If the planet Naptune is 30 AU from the Sun, how many miles is this?

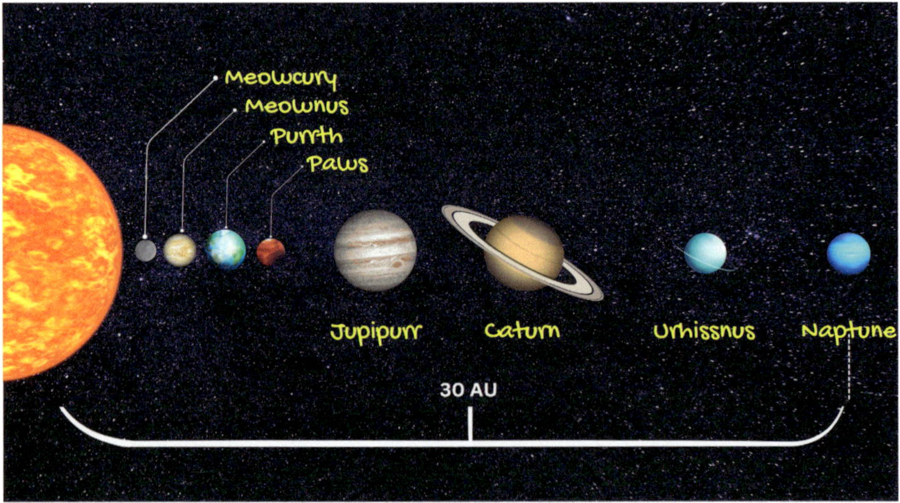

b. If Meowcury is 36 million miles away from the Sun, how many AU is this? Please round your answer to one decimal place.

3. The Moon has much less mass than Purrth, so objects on the Moon weigh less than they do on Purrth. A catronaut travels from Purrth to the Moon. On Purrth, he weighs 12 pounds, but on the Moon, he weighs only 2 pounds.

a. If a cat weighs 9 pounds on Purrth, how much would she weigh on the Moon? Please write your answer as a fraction in its lowest terms.

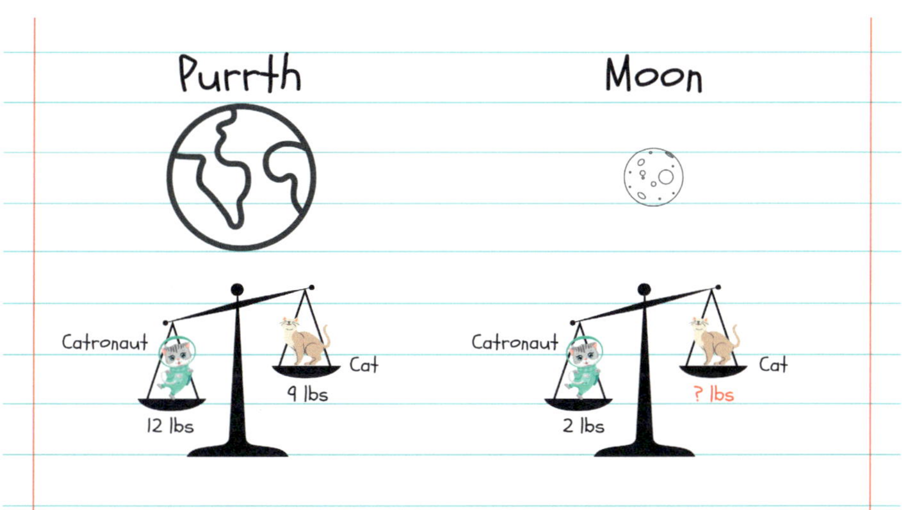

b. How much would the same cat weigh on Naptune if the ratio between the weight of an object on Purrth to that on Naptune is 1 to 1.19? Please round your answer to one decimal place.

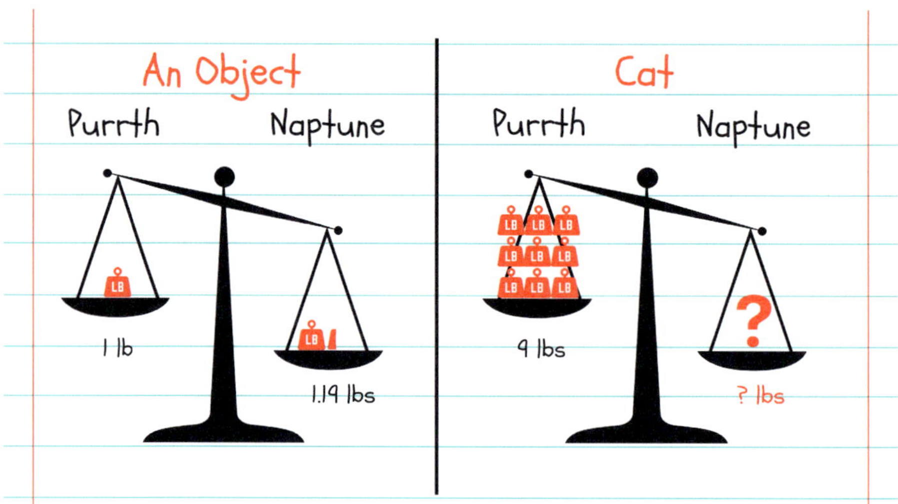

4. When planets are seen close together in the night sky, it is called a conjunction. In a simple solar system, three planets, A, B, and C, revolve around their star, as depicted in the diagram, starting in a lined-up configuration with their star. If planet A takes 2 years to complete one revolution, planet B takes 3 years to complete one revolution, and planet C takes 5 years to complete one revolution, answer the following questions:

a. After how many years will planets A and B line up in conjunction?
b. After how many years will planets A and C line up in conjunction?
c. When will all three planets come into conjunction?

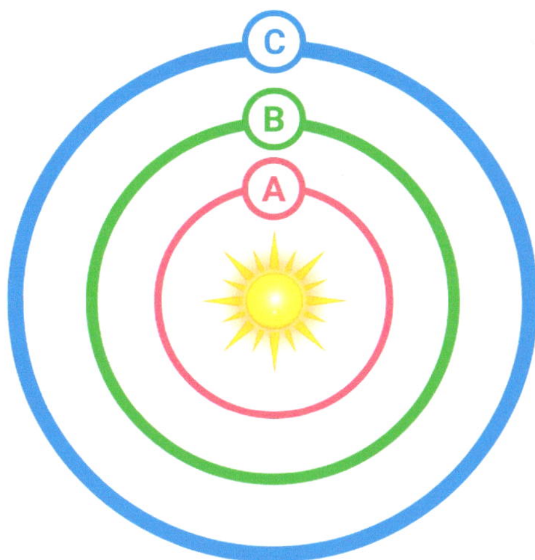

5. A friendly alien cat species visits Purrth to deliver a message. Below are the clues to what the statement says. Use your math skills to decipher the message. Each answer corresponds to a letter shown in brackets at the end of each question. Write the letter corresponding to each answer on the blank lines below to reveal the secret message!

a. 55% of 180 = ____ **(A)**

b. Write 30% as a decimal. **(N)**

c. If Marvin ate one-quarter of a mice-meat pie and Dusty ate three-quarters of another mice-meat pie, how much pie do they have left over between them? **(F)**

d. If Flash the Cat can run 60 miles in 2 hours, how many hours does it take him to reach the next town, which is 120 miles away? **(S)**

e. Buffy scored 18.5 out of 20 on her latest math test. What percent is this? **(M)**

f. If Dusty ate 4 fish-flavored breath mints out of a package, what fraction of the package did he eat if one package contains 12 mints? **(H)**

g. If you have 12 quarters, how many whole dollars do you have? **(T)**

h. 50 is 100% of what number? **(I)**

i. 10 x (9 – 3) + 1 = ____ **(U)**

ANSWER KEY:

1. 8 years

2. a. 2,790,000,000 miles = 2.79 billion miles **b.** 0.4 AU

3. a. 1½ pounds **b.** 10.7 pounds

4. a. 6 years **b.** 10 years **c.** 30 years

5.

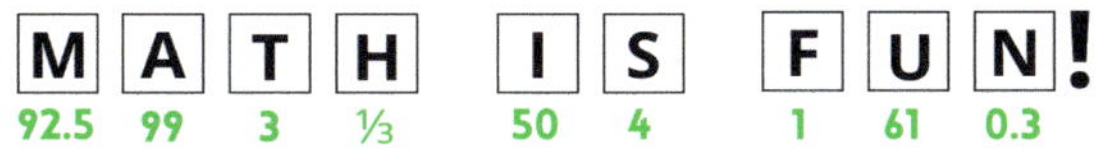

Math Concepts Covered in this Book: Number Sense

1. Ratios: A ratio is a comparison between two or more things. It is similar to a fraction, which expresses the relationship between two numbers by dividing one number by the other. For example, if there are 3 fish-shaped cat treats and 5 mouse-shaped cat treats, the ratio of fish-shaped to mouse-shaped cat treats is 3:5, read 3 to 5.

2. Rates: A rate is a ratio used to compare two different things with different units. For example, how do we determine how fast a car is traveling? If we know the distance a car travels in miles and how long it takes to get to a destination, we can use this information to compute the car's speed in miles per hour (mph). A unit rate is a rate in which the denominator is 1. For example, if a car travels 30 miles in one hour, the unit rate is 30 mph. To solve rate problems, you can use unit rates to compare different rates.

3. Equivalent Ratios and Proportions: Equivalent ratios are ratios that have the same value. In other words, they are equal to each other. When two ratios are equivalent, they can also form a proportion. A proportion is an equation that states that two ratios are equal. For example, 2/3 and 4/6 are equivalent ratios because they both represent the same amount in different ways. This can also be written as a proportion:

$$\frac{2}{3} = \frac{4}{6}$$

To show that these are equivalent ratios, you can multiply or divide both the numerator and denominator of the fraction by the same number. If you divide by 2 on the top and bottom, you can see that both sides of the equation equal 2/3:

$$\frac{2}{3} = \frac{4 \div 2}{6 \div 2}$$
$$= \mathbf{\frac{2}{3}}$$

4. Fractions: A fraction is a way of showing a part of a whole or a group. The top number is called the numerator, and it shows how many parts of the whole we are considering. The bottom number is called the denominator, showing the total number of parts of the whole. To add or subtract fractions, we need to make sure they have the same denominator, called a common denominator. The common denominator in the example below is 6 because both denominators can divide into it evenly. Therefore, we can multiply ⅔ by 2 in the numerator and denominator to get a common denominator of 6:

$$\frac{2}{3} + \frac{1}{6} = ?$$
$$\frac{2 \times 2}{3 \times 2} + \frac{1}{6} = ?$$
$$= \frac{4 + 1}{6}$$
$$= \mathbf{\frac{5}{6}}$$

To simplify or convert a fraction to its lowest terms, divide the numerator and denominator by the same number to make a smaller equivalent fraction. To do this, you need to find the largest number that divides into both the numerator and denominator, called the greatest common factor:

$$\frac{4 \div 2}{6 \div 2} = \frac{\mathbf{2}}{\mathbf{3}}$$

5. Least Common Multiple: The least common multiple (LCM) is the smallest number that two or more numbers can both divide into without any remainders. It is useful in solving problems involving fractions, ratios, and rates. To find the LCM, you can list the multiples of each number and find the smallest one they all have in common. For example, to find the LCM of 2 and 4, we can list their multiples and look for the smallest multiple that is in both lists:

$$2: 2, 4, 6, 8, \ldots$$
$$4: 4, 8, 12, 16, \ldots$$
$$\boldsymbol{The\ LCM = 4}$$

6. Percent: Percent means "per hundred" and is used to express a number as a fraction of 100. For example, 60% means 60 out of 100 or 0.60. To find the percent of a number, you can multiply the number by the percent as a decimal:

$$20\%\ of\ 100$$
$$= 0.20\ \times 100$$
$$= \mathbf{20}$$

To work backward and find the original number, you can divide the given number by the percent as a decimal or use equivalent ratios to figure out the unknown. For example, if you know that 20% of a number is 40, you can divide 40 by 0.20 to find the original number.

7. Order of Operations: When we solve a math expression, we need to follow the order of operations, which tells us what to do first, second, third, and so on. We use the acronym BEDMAS to remember the order: Brackets first, Exponents next, then Division and Multiplication (do them from left to right), and lastly, Addition and Subtraction (do them from left to right too). By following the order of operations, we can get the same answer as anyone else who solves the same math problem. For example:

$$5 \times 4 + (3 + 1 - 2) = ?$$

To solve this problem, do the addition and subtraction from left to right inside the brackets first. Then multiply 5 x 4 to get 20, and finally, add 20 and 2 to get 22:

$$5 \times 4 + (3 + 1 - 2) = ?$$
$$5 \times 4 + (4 - 2) = ?$$
$$5 \times 4 + (2) = ?$$
$$\mathbf{20 + 2 = 22}$$

Acknowledgments

We would like to express our heartfelt appreciation to everyone who has contributed to the creation of this book. First and foremost, we would like to thank Heather's mother and her graduate school friend for their invaluable feedback and suggestions during the editing process. We couldn't have done it without you!

We would also like to thank ToonBoxStudio.com for their excellent online course on drawing cartoon cats, which was instrumental in bringing Marvin and Dusty to life.

Finally, we owe a special debt of gratitude to Spartacus and Keisha, the real-life cats who continue to inspire characters in the *Marvin the Math Cat* book series. Their unique quirks and personalities added life to our feline friends on the pages of this book.

Thank you all for your support and encouragement throughout this journey. We hope *Marvin the Math Cat and Dusty's Secret Quest* will inspire a love of learning and curiosity in young readers everywhere.

About the Author

Heather and Nick Blackburn are an innovative and accomplished couple from Canada's East Coast, who are passionate about creating engaging, educational stories for children. Combining their backgrounds in education, mathematics, astronomy, and computer technology, they bring their expertise to life in their educational children's book series. Alongside their rescue cats, Spartacus and Keisha, they created Marvin the Math Cat, a brilliant feline who takes readers on exciting mathematical adventures. Their award-winning series includes *Marvin the Math Cat and the Mysterious Patio Garden* and *Marvin the Math Cat & Dusty's Secret Quest*, which explores math in the solar system. The Blackburns are committed to continuing Marvin and Dusty's journey of discovery and introducing more children to the practical and exciting world of mathematics. Beyond writing, Heather and Nick enjoy nature walks, yoga, weightlifting, and spending time with their furry feline friends.

facebook.com/marvinthemathcat

https://twitter.com/MarvinMathCat

youtube.com/@marvinthemathcat

instagram.com/marvinthemathcat/

Also By H & N Blackburn

Marvin the Math Cat & the Mysterious Patio Garden

Made in United States
Troutdale, OR
05/04/2024